A Moonlit Teahouse

Anthology of Sacred Poetry

First published in 2015 by
Ninash Foundation   501(c)(3)
17 Center St.
Oneonta, NY 13820
http://www.ninash.org

ISBN 978-0-9829141-3-7

All profits from the sale of this book will benefit
the Ninash Foundation

Designed by Priya Shah
Cover Image © Priya Shah
Illustrations © Priya Shah

A Moonlit Teahouse would like to offer a special thank you to
Krzysztof Lenk for his insights and assistance in bringing this anthology
to fruition.

Contents

a
moonlit
teahouse

Introduction
by Ivan M. Granger

I'd fall silent
-- If only I could --
but this marvel
> *makes my heart leap,*
> *it leaves me open mouthed*
> *like a fool,*

urging me
> *to summon words*
> *from my silence.*

~ Symeon the New Theologian (10th century)

It is the job of theologians, philosophers, and scientists to precisely define the human experience of reality. Most of us simply accept those definitions. A rare few catch the glow pouring through the cracks. We call these strange people visionaries, mystics... poets.

To these explorers, a thing is not a thing, but the light upon it. Yet visionary poets face a unique dilemma: Words themselves are things, discreet packages of meaning. How can one contain the numinous in something so fixed as a word? It can't be done.

Seeing this, some fall silent. Some summon words from their silence. And they write poetry.

Where prose describes and defines, poetry implies. Poetry allows meaning to gather and expand. This elastic quality makes poetry the natural language of sacred experience.

That strand of poetic literature, sacred poetry, has, over the centuries, become a rich multi-cultural conversation in song. *A Moonlit Teahouse* is a delightful part of that continuing dialog. Reading the poems of these modern visionaries and mystics, I find hints of Rumi, Ramprasad, and Rilke, the passion of Mirabai, the roguish wisdom of Han Shan.

--

I should explain some of the history behind this "teahouse" of poets.

Several years ago I founded the Poetry Chaikhana as an online place to explore sacred poetry from around the world. A chaikhana is a Central Asian teahouse. These teahouses are especially associated with the Silk Road, the ancient route used by countless merchants, pilgrims, and travelers. The Silk Road chaikhana would draw in the wise and road-weary from all points of the compass. I began to imagine the teahouse as a gathering place, a place to brush off the dust from the road, a place to sing songs of the journey and of its end. And, of course, in this teahouse, we pass around that most rare brew, the sweet but piping-hot tea of spiritual bliss.

The Poetry Chaikhana first took shape as a website, an eclectic resource featuring the historical poetry of Sufi sheikhs, Christian saints, Hindu rishis, and Buddhist sages. I didn't, however, want to encourage the notion that only the ancients had anything valid to say about spiritual experience. As a way to give voice to contemporary sacred poetry, I soon added an online forum to the website. Very quickly a core group of regular contributors formed, posting their comments, insights, jokes, and, of course, their wonderful poetry.

The forum quickly took on a life and purpose of its own, separate from the rest of the Poetry Chaikhana website. It became clear that I should step aside as the nominal host and moderator in order to let this special community of poets grow in its own direction. While I refocused the Poetry Chaikhana on the poetry of the great sacred traditions, that core circle of forum poets formed their own poetry "teahouse."

This collection, *A Moonlit Teahouse*, is just a sample of the wonderful vision and verse that has emerged from that community of poets. I hope it is only the first of several anthologies to come.

We are so lucky that these poets decided to summon words from their silence.

Ivan M. Granger
Boulder, Colorado

Ann Waddicor

Originally British, and now living in Norway for many years, Ann Waddicor was educated in the fine arts and has lived as a water colour painter, decorator of porcelain (with fine nibbed pen), photographer, and writer of books. Nature, especially trees, is her passion and her hobbies include music and dance, fencing and walking in the mountains.

"I have fenced for my county in GB; swam for my school; danced on a stage; taken control in a glider; walked the Klettersteigen in the Dolomites; visited the Maya Temples in Guatemala; lived six months in Bordeaux, a month in Ravenna; 9 years married in Devon; lived 40 years in Norway, bought my own house in the mountains here; broadcasted to the world's shipping about painting Easter eggs; learned Norwegian folk songs."

Winter's Touch

Not snow
but frost with wings
of glittering silver
stir the grasses, roots,
and dying leaves with white,
in night's lamp—lit glow;
they sparkle, diamonds,
rich beyond compare,
their stiffened forms
made sculptures
by the air,

their gnarled shapes
intensified,
the fingers of the twigs
are glazed with light,
the ground is paled,
and crunches underfoot;

the stars shine extra bright
in atmosphere so clear,
the northern star,
impaled on branches bare,
the silent stare of passers by
so cold,
tucked into scarves
and woollen hats,
and winter coats;

such is this eve

of early winter's fall
so beautiful,
so fierce,
it pierces our concern
for temperature,
the nose drips constantly,
the fingers shiver,
the dark is
in control.

Vernal Wrecks

Crossed twigs, cracked limbs,
a nose protruding, granite mossed
sarcophagus lid, stark Winter's drought,
spilt seed pods black, antler shapes,
bones brittle, broken, bleached,
brown leaves, layered maps,
the season's robbing sap.

Bleating streams scream,
cleaned out frosted roots,
bleeding reds of fallen beasts,
scoured lake, blank face paled,
impaled bark, feathered fringes faded.

Fathoms deep, all sleeps,
weep drops of dew, sharp light, white,
wizened fronds, bracken blackened,
patterned ponds shallow,
dark moulds, mounds, abrupt sounds,
echoes cold across the waste.

Howl wolf, bark fox, squeak mouse,
cackle crow, sigh curlew slow,
torn, seared, smeared, driven,
blizzard tossed, iniquitous,
relentless vernal equinox.

Eye in the clouds

In the sky where you found my eye
this morning—
Magritte had painted it
on a shell of vapour which changed shape in slow motion,
once round
it elongated and finally disintegrated,
becoming one with the whole of the universe,
not gone.

And thus it was dispersed
was free as air
to contemplate the earth, and all its natural phenomena,
without taking part in the human theories and creeds;
clear sighted and innocent like the unwritten slab of stone
before the runes,
or Syrian, Egyptian sculptors
carefully hammered in their words of wisdom,
or the barter of their wares.

And there in the vapours of my mind
formed poems, prose and thoughts,
provoked by the harsh beauty of this planet of blue and white
that, decorated, revolves in space's black abyss.

I kiss the earth, she shudders not,
this Gaia spinning free
and yet she acknowledges me,
so small a cog in the wheel of man's endeavours
constantly sleeping and waking with her every turn.

She laughs at us, our cycles' path of being,
as dawn is dawning all the time
around her ample bosom
and the bread and wine she gathered from space
to furnish us with the possibility of life;
so doing she gave breath to her throbbing heart
controlled and beautiful; her surface layer,
her make-up for the few million years we now exist
perhaps to one day not exist!

No more will any other planet stay, they spin and spin
forever changing in the great wide unending puzzle
that space provides for man to wonder at,
his art, his learning, all, is far away in infinity where
no man can ever reach the limits
unending fires of light and dark,
like fireworks in the skies of many universes,
or so 'they' say!

And should we find out ...all,
will all arts stop up,
will all become so taken for granted, dull?
Or will we reach even greater heights of wisdom,
greater distances into the,
as yet,
unknown future,
a future that is never in the now?

Anna Ruiz

After an experience of cosmic unity in 2005, poetry was reborn. I've been writing ever since to my delight and endless fascination and gratitude to my muse, love and life.

Only
the bare tree
can surrender her last
leaf

It is so written

you take my soul
you dip me in Magellan Blue
with utmost care

for you have found my hiding place
behind an ancient timepiece
shamed into abeyance
where shadows reach not.

Now you wring me out with both your
hands, strong and chiseled
I feel your purpose

you have made me ready.

Now you write, this fine perfect
writing tool I am
my feet a feathertip, I am the swirl
of your letters, the crosses of your words,

Oh, what writing we write!

And now
the parchment yellows
it crumbles in your hands

it blows away in your exhale..

Return me gently
to my hiding place,

you have used me well.

mostly I am lonely just before it rains

we were solitary whales once
oceans ago,
weeping

mostly
I am lonely
just before it rains
just before the sky and I
are so saturated
we must break open
like fireflies
in a child's small, curious hands

pouring

as if there is no tomorrow
no ark
no two by two

drowning

wondering
how we can save each other
from all that rain

small wingless creatures

we come into this world small wingless creatures,
and someone washes us of our mother's blood,
we cry out
and open our lungs to breathe
and somehow a tiny fist is large enough
to hold fast a parent's heart,
strong enough to form loose bonds
that will tear apart mind and body,
wrest a spirit from a soul,
and life is lived
in the loam of earth
on the broken back of selfish dreams

a dreamer must awaken before
the mouth is frozen in silence

and the blood dries with the spittle
and the days are counted in stone.

Black and White

You were the color of smoke
once
when I was a dream of lucidity and
you were a heron flying
so dangerously close,

And
I touched your wings
with
my last breath
as green ice petals
melted
in the deep blue morning,

the death angel praying darkly
hovering
unsure
and we became butterflies in
holy amazement
when
the dragons of time settled down
into the rocks
and sea,
and the sea
returned to infinity,

we rested

and somehow became a dot of black, of white
and these dots

stretched into horizons
and these horizons became stripes
blurring in the distance,

fleet-footed on our zebra feet.

Lemmings

I want to write love poems and
tell you stories of why the Edelweiss
yodel, how your tongue speaks fluently
in my mouth, but it was raining in my dream,

there is no famine in Somalia,
and Palestine is no longer occupied,
I want to spread the word that love has been found
in the shadow-world of man,
the alien has landed
and lives with both feet on the ground,

weapons of mass destruction are buried under
lilies of the field, angry gods no longer speak
and the grasp of a newborn's hand is stronger
than what we have denied in what we leave behind,
hobbling out of Plato's cave on our march to the
endless sea.

salt doll, stone angel and love

undaunted by swift arrows
a gazelle leaps
back into my heart
and the blue heron lifts me
with wings of ecstasy,
a god has awakened

now, where was I, oh,
I am writing a poem
about three lonely serpents
in the garden of good and evil,
everything is glowing
in eleven hundred shades of green,
it is raining softly or maybe my tears
are falling and the sea
ruins me

or maybe it is the story of a painting
inside one amazing brushstroke waiting
to be surrendered:
the devil's brilliant art
and god's manifestation
dying into sound
into the word,
into love

come, my Beloved
loosen your tongue and
die with me,
everything is dying

and the light
is love
and the water
seeks us.

Ashok Kumar Malhotra

Dr. Ashok Kumar Malhotra is a Distinguished Teaching Professor at the State University of New York at Oneonta. He is a romantic rationalist who believes that each one of us is born to do something unique, positive and significant, that we are here to make the world a better place so that we can live our lives with a joyous embrace. He expresses his inner urge for this kind of betterment through the creation of poetry, paintings, and books on philosophy, religions and yoga as well as through the "Yoga Life" column he writes for the *O'Town Scene of the Daily Star* and through his work to establish the Ninash Foundation (www. ninash.org), a charity that builds elementary and high schools for impoverished female and minority children of India.

From the collection

"Tears from the Heart"

Celebration of Life

Two beings isolated by nothingness!

A physical separation,
An uncanny situation,

An imaginary aberration,
A mental creation,

Then with a startling flash,
Without doubt or mental clash,

Cognition of one's other self,
Self's unison with the self,

Insight struck that this is the one,
Realization that I and you are spiritually one!

Two equals in temporal companionship,
A model for eternal relationship!

Darkness and light
Blended in a rainbow!

Two rivers of life
Merged in a confluent flow!

Dancing
To the music of spheres,

Today, tomorrow and eternally
Without angst or fear!

Symbolizing Love

The lover's attempt at symbolizing love!
In the form of a flying dove,
The sign of eternal peace,
When the two souls are at ease!
In the form of a pierced heart,
Injured by an arrow or a dart!
In the form of two hearts in an embrace,
Becoming one and yet keeping their unique face.
In the form of a smooching kiss,
So perfectly fitting that nothing is amiss.
In the gentle holding of hand,
Walking in the air
Without touching the land!
In thinking of the other as a mystery,
Realizing her unique story and history!
For centuries attempts have been made,
Under the candle light and sun's shade,
To symbolize love
As a throbbing heart
Jumping out of the rib cage
Or as a love letter
Written on an infinite page,
Displaying it to be an extraordinary experience
In which everyone ought to engage.

"Celebration of Life": Previously published in Best Poems of 1998, The National Library of Poetry

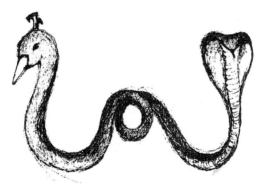

Rainbow and Rain

Human beings are prone to complain!
When there is too much or too little
snow or rain!
I tell them
it is foolish to complain
because how could there be a rainbow without rain!
How could there be appreciation
of life's joys
if there was no pain!
How could there be a sunrise
without its counterpart of sunset?
Is not it futile
then to be upset?
How could there be victory
without defeat?
How could there be a rainbow without the rain?
How could there be birth of life without pain?
How could you admire light
without
its counterpart of darkness?
How could there be rainbow without the rain?
Birth and death; darkness and light;
pleasure and pain; sadness and delight;
all exist side by side;
without crushing the other's right!
Let's embrace the opposites
without offering resistance or fight;
because how could birth happen without any pain
and how could there be a rainbow without the rain!

Previously published in The Best Poems and Poets of 2007, The National Library of Poetry

Barry Abate

Born into the New Jersey suburbia of the 50's, and greatly
influenced by the new trends in music and poetry, I became
keenly aware of the sad world I had been born into. Poetry gave
me a way of expressing the joys and shortcomings of being all
too human in a world we are only momentary travelers in.

factory

I loved into the loss of my hands the weeping hours
the tongue creaked door closed on what I made
the dark ghost of cornered light
dreaming a commodity of hopes
the conformity of my fingers
became sky again
not solid or made tangible
a tree conformed to planks in the repetition of the blade
the soil held in the smelter's vision
I release in time these hard held atoms.

lover's rain

when the earth turns its face to fire
less dark beside me you lay

feeding the morning into your mouth
you swallow and grow light

when i reach

you wander from my bed
into the heart of every lover
shy in clouds you feed me with trees
and flow into me with tongues of mountains

you return to me in pools of water
then
i know the night hunger before you are fed

i reach again into your raining eyes
and you pour into me a parting cloud

such a deeper truth i entered
at your return
transforming me into your lover again

and i touched you again as your moon dress fell
upon the water my eyes gave you

filling my mouth with yours
you rain into me all things growing
alive and together completely

the planting

If they come
(each moment dancing on the pin of my thoughts);
you would have come
bringing them
the lost hours
the exact fuddle of my fingers
to that extreme intensity
the contoured bridge along the towering fragment love
whereupon passes the belly
of my soul
and we growing together
in arches
the plant of all my gardens,
the lost way home
to this I have gathered
all the stones to my feet
in the numbness of alone walking
to the foot of the last wall
and the felled tree

moon cactus

it is not eyes
or hand or reach
that follows you
prickling as a cactus
into the desert of dry years

it is when night is most alone
in a song for the shadows
the moon leaves behind
when you did not know anything
but were more held than reason
in the palm of each leaf
that never asked you to be anything
but silent

Cloud of Unknowing

Cloud of Unknowing is a writer living in Kansas.

Blasphemous Grace

I lose myself in Your manifestations
My wife and my lovers
Their napes, lips, breasts, hips
Angles of spacetime
Their tender points
Deep singularities
The songs of my women
When they find themselves
Bend galaxies

What blasphemous liturgy
Has brought me to this state of grace?
Lost within these vibrations
Inside of God

The Secret Religion

At night I worship
Fire at my feet
Rising, centered,
I beg Her to
Burn me away
I beg

She draws me in
Until there is nothing of me
But a point of love
Revolving around Her Gravity

This is a terrible poem. . .
How can I describe what it is like
To be taken apart
Bit-by-bit, atom-by-atom
Every night
By the Woman who is all women?

Only those who have dared caress Her
Who have blasphemed strongly enough to
Taste Her nectar
Can know My Secret Religion

How Can I Deny You?

How can I deny you?
For three weeks now I have felt your touch
Raging bliss and
Fire within and
Gentle love;

Stroking the locks of my hair
Is a secret lover, God Herself within me
Love made tangible
Heat radiant
Shaking with joy
I Tremble with desire for more You
How can I deny You?
Take me and do with me as You please
How can it be otherwise?

CS Thompson

CS Thompson is the author of *Prayers for Nothing*, *The Wind Between the Worlds*, and the *Noctiviganti* novels.

www.noctiviganti.com

No Resting Place

I was told in the Borderlands that I should seek no resting place,
That we accept no serenity, because the flowerlike face
Of the Almighty Sorrow is a yearning, an ache—
That God Himself is imperfect, and in fact, God is heartbreak.

Faith

If I could just have seen what lay behind,
Beyond the walls, and past the other shore
Where they assured me God's true glory shined—
A light that even I could not ignore.

And yet they never opened up the door
But kept me waiting in another room,
Attending on the loom of peace and war—
I let the Old One swallow me too soon.

And I can never say that I was sure...

Spiritual Materialism

I hungered for the silver light
Of those who walk the moon.
They never showed their wings that night
Or else they came too soon.

I hungered for the sudden tears
That meant the sun was mine.
I waited for a hundred years,
But missed the proper time.

On bended knee I sought the source
Of all that moves above,
And only when I knew remorse
Decided it was love.

Hedieh Sajadi aka Darya

The first time ever I wrote a poem was when I lost my mother. I had no idea where all those words were coming from, and I could not even explain their presence in that desperate and sad time of my life. In the midst of the tears and sorrow I seek refuge in my pen. The words kept pouring on me like rain and they were my only companions in those lonely cold days. Time, however, made me think less about my sorrow and more about the life I was going to have ahead of me. After all I was only a teenager. So eventually the wounds started to heal and I no longer felt or needed the presence of words in my life.

But then came the day that I fell in love. The feeling was amazingly beautiful and innocently beyond this world. Words, those old companions of mine, one by one started to show up in my heart. They became in charge and made me write nothing but Love. It is true that you only fall in love once and you can never fall out of it.

The world of poetry eventually became my sanctuary and a place to worship my beloved. It became THE SEA of hidden emotions and desires. I had no choice then but to choose the pen name *Darya*.

And now I no longer even exist. I have become this word itself. My name, whatever that is, will be forgotten anyway like a faded memory that constantly skips the mind, but the word *Darya* represents the state of existence, and it is going to stay with the reader long after I am gone.

e-mail: daryaehabi@yahoo.com

Every morning

Every morning
you pick my poem
from the garden
like a flower
placing it in the crystal vase
by the window

Do you think
sunshine will help it to still grow?
or watching the rain behind the closed window
is going to satisfy its thirst?

For you
it is only good for a few hours
perhaps a day or two
till you toss it out to be buried in the garden

But it is there
in the garden
out of your sight
that it becomes alive
under the shade of that apple tree
where the red ink stains my fingers
it comes back to life

There is no time to repent
it already had molded my soil
into the shape of a bird
flying solo in the air
with no regret

This crowd is drunk

This crowd is drunk

with the wine of self

undesirable poetry

grows profusely where it's not wanted

and I am in search of love

Still

Every night I come to the tavern

like I have no other place to go

a bitter poison vitiates and corrupts my mind

I drink it with the roots of my soul

and I am in search of love

Still

Each time that I open this door

I walk through a seemingly endless time

of no beginning and no ending

it is the absence of truth

and I am in search of love

Still

Every Poem

Why is it that every poem I read
I feel you have written it for me?

How do these floating words
Even find their way to the universe of me?

Have I opened any window to capture your words
Like I am the summer night
That needs to breathe your breeze?

How is it that every word I write
Finds its way to your heart?

Is it because of my imagination
Or is it because of the pain that I felt in your eyes?

Still I wonder
Where are all the words coming from?
Out of nowhere or from the bottom of a broken heart?

To whom do these words even belong?
Are these words yours or mine?

You know... sometimes poetry just comes
Exactly at the moment
That I was going to kiss it goodbye

A 100-year-old chandelier

There is a 100-year-old chandelier here
still lights the house
the floor we have been walking on
has footprints of lovers

Trees have been blossoming
every spring
the same old song has been playing
over and over

In the garden
I think of you
sometimes
when I reach for the apple blossoms
it reminds me of November
the taste of an apple is such a distant memory now
oh... how joyfully I used to bite into one

You have gone
and I have gone
each our own separate ways
yet, still, love is with both of us
at the same time
in the same space...

Teahouse Poem 1

Cutting through
Lotus of a thousand petals
Miracles rise
From the eye of wonder

Again
I think of ruby dawns
And the scarlet letters

The undiminished returns of cherry blossom
Lilies and
Your touch
By the river

Tonight
I am
Silently drawn to you.

Teahouse Poem 3

Rules of conduct no longer apply
For every mean thing
Still
We awaken the sleepy God
Stealing myths
From the blueberries to the bushes

You left a window open
To the way of snow
To the novel of pearls
And
Here appeared she
Like a flower

How beautiful is
The color of light
Jealous lover just
Turn and use my wine

You asked
What is in a poem?
What is the state of the poet?
And what is sacred in Poetry?

I answered
Hafez
The moon
And I ....

Dick Holmes

Born in Kansas, USA, in 1949, Dick Holmes has lived in South Carolina, USA, for most of his adult life. Author of a large collection of poems entitled *Recipes for Gratitude* (Pure Heart Press, www.mainstreetrag.com/DickHolmes.html), he is a featured poet at Poetry-Chaikhana.com (www.poetry-chaikhana.com/H/HolmesDick/index.htm) and at AvatarMeherBaba.org (www.avatarmeherbaba.org/erics/dickholmes.html). Before retiring in March 2011, he made a career of teaching English and English as a second language.

e-mail: dick_holmes@epi.sc.edu

Day 22159

For many years I used to teach English.
Now I'm retired and English is teaching me.
I was born in Kansas near a wheatfield and a crow.
There I learned how to play baseball.
From baseball I learned geometry.
From geometry I learned bread making.
From bread making I learned poetry.
From poetry I'm learning how to unlearn things.
I find I'm happiest when I'm simply being alive.

Dear One

In many a letter—one long,
intermittent one, actually—I've
said so many things to you, though your
real name and who you really are
I know I know only superficially.

On the way to the blueberry field
this afternoon, we hear thunder and
wonder. A thunderstorm wasn't in the
forecast when we checked before we left,
but apparently things have changed—
as if they'd ever stop changing.
We keep going, anyway. The sun
is shining and we might get to
see a rainbow, or the storm might end up
blowing off in another direction and we'll
still get a bucket of blueberries.

The Ever-Clean Slate of Meaning

Like the meaning of ancient glyphs
scratched on a piece of slate
and molecule by molecule swept
completely away after thousands of years
of wind, rain, and sun, what's happened
has happened. The amazing thing is that
that piece of slate still manages
to hang in there, holding its own.
Maybe it's waiting for one more pleasant
backscratching before it bites the dust.

Words for It

We words come
from wherever
for what keeps coming.
In other words,
we never catch up,
though in its wake
we do point to
the loving
silence ahead.

Song of the Flute

Without the holes
in the Great Spirit's reed,
my fingers would atrophy
and my song would be
the gasp of a caged bird.
Without the breath
the Great Spirit
passes through me,
there would be no song at all
to celebrate Its wind.

Language

Yes, Being,
truly,
it's Love
always
leading
the way,
and Love is
what it is
all about,
all there is.

It couldn't be
otherwise.

And language is
a spontaneous
bridge
from Ocean
to Ocean,
from Love
to Love,
Love's
language
for Love.

Dorothy Walters

Dorothy Walters, Ph. D., is a retired university professor (English and Women's Studies) who, at age 53, experienced a dramatic Kundalini awakening which, as she says, completely transformed her life. She had no guru or teacher to guide her through this process, navigating through the new world that opened itself to her by following inner guidance and instinct. In recent years she has published two volumes of spiritual poetry (*Marrow of Flame* and *A Cloth of Fine Gold*) as well as a spiritual biography describing her awakening experience (*Unmasking the Rose*). She publishes a blog at www. kundalinisplendor.blogspot.com that focuses on reflections and poetry of the spiritual path.

e-mail: dorothywalters72@yahoo.com

Sea Change

I do not know
how I got caught up
on this wave,
bounding and tossing,
always farther out to sea,
always being shaped
into a new image,
meanwhile
my other self
watching not so much
in fear
but in curiosity and a casual interest
from the shore,
thinking,
Yes, now I am becoming
who I truly am,
go ahead,
pound and mold me,
make me whatever it is
I am supposed to be
now at this time, in this place,
neither of which is locatable
on time pieces or maps,
both together forming a matrix
constantly shifting,
as if it can't quite make up its mind
where it wants to go,
or else has a purpose
that no one else
can see.

The Angel

And if we should
perceive that
angel,
its shimmering wings,
its blazing hair,
let us have courage
to look
at it fully,
to feel
its radiant energies
as these flow
into who we are,
making us
more than we have
ever been
or imagined.

For an angel
is hard to bear.

What it demands
of us
greater than
the accustomed round.

What it wants
is nothing less
than everything,
relinquishment
of all the old ways,

heart opening
to a new creation,
self refashioned
into a more luminous design.

Awakenings

Some do it quickly,
like making love over
a short noon break,
lightning flash of illumination,
bursting nova
in the brain.

Others take their time,
are sensuous,
meditative,
thoughtfully absorbing for years
the soft rays of love,
relishing each one.

Others try to follow a book
with its stages
and diagrams,
but they get lost
somewhere
between the
many charts
and prescriptions.
Who wants to
try to remember
how to breathe in a certain way
or count the petals of a lotus flower
when
making love?

Best to let it happen

in its own manner,
a sly spirit
winking down
from the ceiling,
a serious lover
come to call
when least expected.

Classic texts describe a perfect model for Kundalini awakening, as the energy moves from the lower to the upper chakras. However, the process seldom follows this ideal prescription, but rather proceeds according to its own unique design and desire.

Eldyheart

Since I was born I have been searching to find my way home to God.

In the Kindness of Your Love

In the kindness of your love
I feel the angels from above
reaching down with gentle wings
kiss my heart that softly sings

So much I do not understand
but by your blessed touch of hand
I open up my deepest place
to let it fill with all your grace

Resting then in safety found
my fears and terror be unbound
the doors of glory open wide
my being does not need to hide

when held by you in sweet embrace
of pain and sorrow no more trace
and when the music starts to play
I know you'll never go away

I know the union through the bliss
will always cover all I miss
and fill and heal with all its might
that only loves and has no fright

cause through this journey of despair
the threats will shake us all with fear
the losses seem so real and cold
like our souls were left and cold

like God forgot us here on Earth
to let us suffer from our birth

and then we dream and hope and try
that what can save us will come by

and torn in pain and broken in fear
I cried so loud to God up there
please take me, let me go away
cause I don't have the strength to stay

my life has been a walk on edge
my heart was crying out the pledge
please, let this world be free
and help me, dearest God, to see

that there can be a way of Love
that there are angels high above
that Love is stronger than all fear
that all your children are you dear

that you will keep us in your hand
and we rejoice that you are grand
and our being you restore
to heaven open up the door

and let us be what we were meant
from you your angels you have sent
to come with glory and delight
and you will heal us with your light

and we are home and we are whole
and you will fill our cup and bowl
and keep us safely held as Thine
our eyes and heart filled with Thy Shine.

Amen.

Night Garden in Bloom

Precious beyond comprehension.
Beams of Light into my garden of night.
Long forgotten seeds sleeping under soil.
Dreaming flowering that never came to be.

Then a moment outside and inside time.
I see you. Glowing Light talking me to Life.
Patterns of unfolding recognizing its key.
Cascading energy opening paths of growth.

Dancing heavenly winds celebrate in the garden.
Ready now, sweet nectar of deepest Love.
There are flowers everywhere. A sound of joy.
And the heart is a red rose opening to the Beloved.

You Sing Me Again to Be

long journey of despair
in darkness no path anywhere
my tired steps in lonely land
feeling no one in my hand

the dreams of tender light
companion in silent night
where shadows rested near
this heart full of fear

desperate call in forest deep
hurting and no more tears to weep
the music I longed for never came
no one knew my name

and then this verse for you
who sent your light in me through
what was left of me, and to see
you sing me again to be

into the deep of me you go
the long-forgotten song plays now
I open this morning as new
my whole being singing you

Fatima

Feeling the blessing of the divine
I surrender to the beauty that could only befit God.
Such wonder, sublime, such splendor, and awe
I lose myself in the glory of the Mahdi, I find me, Ya Mahdi

http://www.facebook.com/fatima.azher

cry me a river

Call up what you think, the theories you concoct
And I'll tear them down
Sing me your songs, of meaningless words and dead instruments
And I'll burn you out of tune

Cry me a river, I swear I won't have pity
Be you calling upon me, I shall not answer, no.

But believe… believe in the sheer beauty of God
And I shall love you. Love you for the love of God
Watch the signs of God, immerse yourself in the power of purity
And I shall immerse myself in you, you as you become a sign from God.

I shall love no other… none but whose hand the Hand of God
Places in mine. I can not love—aught but God
It's not that I don't care…
It's just that I care too much
And the depths of care cry out…
Weep…
For God.
God.
And God Alone.

Make me come alive

there is an image in my eye
grandeur resounding in my ears
there's a voice upon my lips
that isn't really mine

who is it i'm in love with?
who dwells upon my mind
who is this God has taken over me?
who is this i love, whom i can not reach?
who is this reaching unto me, who is this

who is this that teaches me
the language of my own heart
who is this piecing together my fragmented soul?
who is this that insists upon holding me by the hand
when i would rather close my eyes and fall in slumber
who is this—this bringer of love and frenzy,

a catalyst for the breath of life, a stranger to the dark
who is this that insists... will make me come alive?

Ivan Granger

Ivan M. Granger is the creator and editor of the *Poetry Chaikhana* web site, www.Poetry-Chaikhana.com. He grew up in Oregon and Southern California, and has lived on the island of Maui. He now lives in Colorado with his wife.

When asked why he writes poetry, Ivan says, "Poetry has an immediate effect on the mind. The simple act of reading poetry alters thought patterns and the shuttle of the breath. Poetry induces trance. Its words are chant. Its rhythms are drum beats. Its images become the icons of the inner eye. Poetry is more than a description of the sacred experience; it carries the experience itself."

e-mail: ivan@poetry-chaikhana.com

How can I explain

Beloved, they want to know:
Did I reach up to You,
or did You reach out to me?

And they want to know:
What is real
touch?

How can I explain
we pour
into each other?

There Is No Letting Go

There is no
letting go.

Even your absence
touches me.

The new moon
is not gone;
she hides
her face
   in the night.

The Warbler Knows

The warbler knows
only dawn's shaft
of light
on her breast.

Forgetting false future
suns, she sings

in no voice
but her own.

Originally published May 2010 in TIFERET: A Journal of Spiritual Literature *(www. tiferetjournal.com)*

Games in a green field

Games in a green field,
children at noon. The only
quiet—my shadow.

Jake Murray

Jake Murray has been a poet since he was a teenager, when he was a Shell Commended Young Poet in 1986 and a Charterhouse Shortlist Poet in 1989. He took up writing again a few years ago and has since found the experience an absolute delight, as well as a key part of his days.

Since writing again, Jake has had five poems published in the *Decanto Poetry Magazine* and was runner up in last year's British Writers Awards.

Jake's favorite poets are T S Eliot and William Wordsworth, who have probably inspired and influenced him the most, with Eliot's "Four Quartets" his most evergreen poem, having stayed with him for over twenty years. He also loves Shelley, Gerard Manley Hopkins and the great Medieval English mystic poet, William Langland.

For Jake, poetry remains unashamedly about magic, about the Spirit, about love, about beauty and about hope. The traditional vocation of the poet as singer is still alive to him. In an increasingly dark and cynical world, the song is needed.

From the collection

"JAPA"

Teahouse

The hot mists of the morning
Rise from the lake in the mountains.
Green leaves, ripe and oily dip
In the early rain. The sky can be seen,
Swathed in clouds, from the earth. Birds,
Like splashes of colour, cry from the
Undergrowth, bright plumes appearing
And disappearing in the
Shadows.

         By the water, a wooden
House sits. Duckboards snake beside
The ripples from the cool wetness
Of the waves. No-one is speaking,
But someone is waiting, sat cross-
Legged by the doorway, a mat
Beneath his knees. He greets you,
Smiles and lifts his head to draw
You into the chamber;
                On the floor,
China cups in blue and white; beside
Them, the greenest tea.

Petworth

Out here, beneath the trees, in the garden
Among the green, I feel the wind lift the leaves
And lift them again, like a prayer.

I sense the air rise beneath the branches, hear
Them whispering, caressing me, speaking
Their long-worn wisdom of comfort as I wait.

The day is grey, but not cold. The rain has
Ceased and I am released from the house
To take part in this. There is calm here, there is calm.

I wait and watch. In the distance, the drowsing
Countryside stretches away to hills. Houses
Rest by the wayside. People live and breath.

I feel them all. The flowing horizon of hedges
And fields has stood like this forever.
The wind catches the leaves again.

I hear them. I hear them.

Shakti

She dances for him
In the failing light
By the sea-shore
Waves beating
Breaking her heart
For the lover she loves

And he watches
Lost in the smoothness
Of her arm and legs
The curve of thighs
The flow of skin
Song sung

Together
Beneath the stars
And as she dances
They move apart,
Distance spreading
So far and gone

Forever wandering
Looking again
For the sea shore.
Lost among men
Lost among women
Strangers in streets

That cover the sea
Forget the song

Conceal the memory
Of the dancing self
Beneath the sky
But somewhere

She dances for him
In the failing light
By the sea-shore
Waves beating
Breaking her heart
For the lover she loves

Catechism

Let the whole world
  be your church
Let the trees and hills
  be your altar
Let every human face
  be the face of God

Let each day
  be a Sabbath day
Let each stranger
  be an angel
Let each deed you do
  be an act of love

May the sun
  be your joy
May the moon
  be your blessing
May the sky
  be your heaven
May the earth
  be your dwelling

May your life
  be a hymn
May your sleep
  be a song
May your hours
  be rich
May your happiness
  be long

Hypnos

I send you blessings
And kisses for your eyes.
May they rest beautifully tonight.
If you feel wings brush you
As you sleep
It is me, my love,
It is me,
Only me.

I leave flowers on your pillow
To give you fragrance as you dream.
And if you smell petals
As you sigh
In your sleep
It is me, my love,
It is me,
Only me.

Penelope

Her hands move across the fabric
Weaving patterns processing like Time
Through landscapes of gods and monsters.

Palaces rise above mountains,
Heroes cross oceans in ships of gold,
Queens bear treasures, Kings wage wars

As children listen, catching the light
Which pours through the trees,
As stories are told forever.

Her fingers are no longer young.
Creases gather about her eyes and lips,
Hair streaked white and silver like memories,

Each one a day left long with waiting,
Months, years, listening for his tread
That never comes to her door.

She wears his memory like the bedclothes around her.
Athena gathers like a mist by the window.
Time sighs about the room, shifting over blankets,

Consuming thoughts and echoes and dreams
That yawn and ache by the mantle.
Downstairs men laugh and roar as they eat,

Wine and meat and flesh by the fire,
Coarse eyes burning, she dare not dream,

Music and song and ugliness.

As night falls the work begins
Of unravelling the worlds she has created,
Tearing apart the tales she has told

To begin the tapestry anew. Stately face
In the window, lined with pain of years gone by,
She waits, as she has for a lifetime

For him to come and take her,
To feel his arms as she did then,
His man's step crossing the floor.

Jonathan Weiss

Jonathan Weiss is married to the lovely Jacquelynn Weiss. He is the father of four, has two rescued Siamese cats and a rescued Airedale-mix puppy. Dr. Weiss has practiced Dentistry for forty years, plays guitar and keyboards, is a member of the Self Realization Fellowship, and loves to solve any and all forms of the crossword puzzle. His first book of poetry will soon be published, and he has greatly enjoyed being part of this collaboration.

e-mail: jmwddspc@aol.com

Grand Eclipse

To bask in the glorious sun of Your eyes
without being judged, remarkably enough
causes the sunrise itself to lose significance
in the frame of today...

Expedition

Your sweet secret whisper echoes through the ether.
I listen intently through the stillness as my
heart opens, yet cannot fathom its meaning.

Your plan remains beclouded in hieroglyphics,
and deep as I go inside, cannot be deciphered.
It is only through forgetting my mind, and
unearthing my intuition, do I have any hope
of harboring understanding.

The Mystery is blissful—
it can only be dreamed
with an infant's innocence.

Deja Vu

We are the teacher
we are the student
always learning,
always yearning
for wisdom divine
and yet...
it has always been
yours and mine.

A Prayer

Come to me

Shine through me

Undo me

Will You come to me ever
and make me Your own?
The knots will You sever
and let me come Home?

Home where the mercy,
the peace and the joy
will rob my adulthood
and make me a boy.

A child who knows nothing
of worldly endeavor
but plays in the heavens
in love with forever.

All the World

The curtain rises and
a new dream is born—
an opportunity, a direction
and the means to make
it reality.

The actor takes center stage.
Self-assured, clothed in colors
of grandeur, he speaks,
commanding every eye.

His actions are witnessed
with love and respect;
because he portrays the life
of every man ever born.

As he exits stage left,
he changes, leaves the theatre,
hails a cab and continues his
journey, with the cheers of
the audience following him home—

to the next scene.

One Man's Prayer

I hate to see you go
out into winter's desolation,
dragging your sodden shoes—
while dreams of five hundred
flashing suns climb your soaked legs,
past your heavy heart, to reach
your wind-drifted face.

Unfurl your umbrella. Hold it
upside down and catch the
sweetness of spontaneity that splashes up
into your downcast eyes as it washes
away visions of hopelessness—

and floods your fears until you come home
to the greening of fields that sway
left and right, joyful for the rain.
Let your nightmares melt into a mind,
holding the unshakeable peace of knowing who you are.

Max Reif

I was blessed to receive the Grace of Avatar Meher Baba at age 22. Before that, I believed I'd irreparably messed up my life. I turned out to need even MORE help. In 1976, Ram Dass midwifed a certain deep Opening. The poem below says the rest.

"Remembering January 17, 1976,
Downtowner Motel, Oklahoma City."

Remembering

If you could journey in the mind of a saint,
you would go for days and see
only light,

but if you travel
through the mind of a soul in darkness
you won't see a single ray
except possibly the faintest glimmer
from something far, far away.

I've been both places,
garden as a boy, then fallen,
sure as our ancient forbears,
not mere expulsion
but seeming black
damnation

until I entered that room that day
and kindness trained
its eyes upon me

and the soft yet blazing light
found its way across the room
into my eyes and then
like a deft, expanding cat
kept going, gently,
all the way inside.
We emerged

a couple of hours later,
two beams of One
laughing Sun.

The Dance

The Tavern Keeper
offered me a drink
from the Moon's silver chalice.

As I tipped it to my lips,
I prayed, 'O Beauty,
make me like yourself!'

The sky began to dance and whirl,
the hoopskirt of a fragrant woman.
She held my hands
and took me whirling with her.

I danced through the night with Night!

And when morning came,
she turned from whirling
in her dark blue skirt,

and offered me
her rosy face

Predicament

With Your hammer
Coming down on my head,

You want me to
Become a willing nail.

Instead, I run,
Go looking for a helmet
To ward off Your blows.

Where I am now,
All my maps have failed.
You are the only Road

To get me from here
To HERE.

Interfaith

Now, there's something to be said about an event
in a small neighborhood church
that makes the walls give way,
all walls and most especially
the ones in my heart, and puts me
at the center of the cosmos on the first
morning of Creation.

Frankly, I went to hear *our* group,
I mean I went because our group was singing,
but the group that went first
played Indian instruments and sang to Shiva,
sitting in front of the big golden Cross on the altar
with Jesus on it nicely dressed and looking
not at all unhappy.

And that was when I got the hit,
"You don't have to be on guard
or compare your path to theirs,
they're singing to the One
you sing to, it's a little
like calling someone 'Bob' or 'Robert'."

And then when "our" group did come on
I had my eyes closed and instead
of their all marching up onto the stage
and singing *down* at us,
they simply stood up at the end of each row
where they'd been sitting
and I felt surrounded with Love,

like they were inside me, that close,

and I thought "NOW, now is the moment
I enter the New Age!"

A little later we made a huge circle,
holding hands all around the outer aisles
for a Native American dance
of Universal Peace, "May I walk in Beauty,"
and I knew again how important circles
will be in the new age, all-inclusive,
no beginning or end, no above or below.

And I know this kind of Mirror where we all
pray each other's prayers and sing
one another's songs can't help
but leave us feeling, "That's *me* there
in another body and another color shirt,
we're all sincere and all
on the same Journey, there's no
competition only wanting to do
my best to let the Light come through
pure, and rooting for the others
to do that, too, that way there's more
Nectar for everyone!"

Frankly, I never thought Religion could save the world,
but if we all keep doing it *this* way,
how can we miss?

Working on a Poem with George

I told George I'd come over
and help him with his poems,
but by the time I got there
was strung out on sleeplessness
and too much coffee.

He said that was ok
and giving me a glass
of water, led me to the glass
table with a stack
of papers and a pencil
waiting at each end.

He sat at one end,
I at the other,
and here we were,
my mind like a car
revving and dying.

George proceeded calmly,
reading me his lines
that needed work.

My crippled mind fed me ideas
and, nothing else to do
in the vastness there between us,

I passed them on to George.
He tried each out and either settled
for my word or phrase

or used it as a stepping-stone.

He honored both
the silence and the time,
and I began to, too.
I saw that limping, hobbled bird
my mind, begin to hop, and then to fly.

Later, walking out the door,
well-fed by concentration's fires,
my mind and body both

flew from the porch-perch, out
into a startling paradise created
while I'd been indoors.

Spirit blown drunk
by the liquor of the breeze,
my eyes oozed sweet
with seeing's honey.

Michael Firewalker

Michael Firewalker learned to write from the coffeehouse "Beats", the poets of the fifties, who taught hir to write from hir gut, hir soul. Born and raised in historically "blue collar" Tacoma, Washington, s/he is now a retired registered nurse, and has been writing hir own style of poetry for fifty-eight years.

S/he has published one book, *Light-Speak*.

How Mother God Wove Creation

Mother weaves Her lively web
beloved kind from first to last

lightnings race where thunders crash

their broad-edged paths crush their way
through all of space
down all of time

everywhere into the airs She spreads
Her silken perfumed web
descending on Her plaited hair
in burning wires of Goddess fire
she splits new stars
as maelstroms of celestial wars
scatter all across the floors
that hold Her midnight sky

She opens turgid pregnant eyes
where Her beloved cherubs cry
in raptures sung as ecstasy
in purities of bliss they pray
to sanctify the virgin day

they worship distant vaulted powers
unseen in holy hidden towers
until their songs can freely seed
wet gifts of newborn Light
sent down as sprouting tender reeds
dropped into elemental hands

who set them free to breed
across the lands of all the universes

from those grand and glowing seas
there can be seen Spirit rise as spirit Life

while Creation's delight
organizes utility
with all of the infinity
of quantum possibility

then down the darkness of the deep
along the ageless running fall
and way way up the farthest climb
far past the oldest veiled wall
right where Desire stands to call

there commands one single Scarlet Thread:

Rise up and singing from your beds
rise upward now from the dead

come you come I
come one come all
who long to touch Sublime!

come those who will and all who dare
and them who Love from everywhere

look to see and reach to find

yourselves inside Mother's wild
timeless eyes

where circles flat of simplest line
wove spheres wrought deep in detail fine
in webs that kiss the ends of time.

for epochs come and epochs go
and eras seek what eons know
that here on Earth we too will make
perfection's stand

here come we
Creation's children hand in hand
formed from fertile sod
Mother's breath in Jesse's rod

blessed streams
eternal Joy redeemed

fulfillment of all grace and peace

Light become
Love's masterpiece

flames of all-consuming fire
lift now high and higher
and here we come

One song
singing
One

Eagle Remembers

Great Spirit has said
the soul of Eagle runs red
and he sees very far
remembering his own

the high land
the shimmering sky land
has ever been home

from beginning of time
we all know
it is there he has flown

his sisters and brothers
of the two-legged kind
ranged happily far below

they honored the skies
and cared for the seas
respected the animals
protected the trees
moving carefully through
all of their days
nearly all of their ways
born of peace

they walked fine
in body and mind
and their dancing joys ran
like wild berry wine

today as they walk
their bodies seem dead
leaving only their spirits
living instead

while their souls go bodiless
walking this land
blessing, protecting
their still sacred home
they had never presumed to own
like the white men had
when they flooded like locusts
onto the ground
with plough and fence
and bullets in hand
and murdered the families
of Eagle's they found
till over the land
were fearfully spread
so many red skins
of its own native dead

silent they lay
in a great quilted band
sad tribute indeed
to greed
hunger and dread

for centuries
Eagle

had watched
from above

he heard all the killing
he felt all the pain
it rose in the air
like upside-down rain

and also there came
upward the cries
of the two-legged families
with whom he had grown
whose strong braves had fought
the "Indian wars" far below

he watched as defeated they walked there
on those long trails weeping to nowhere
sickly and starving they came
force-marched over the land

weighed down right to the end
by the white man's shame
till at last there were few
who were able to stand

now many long years
passed sadly on by
then one fine day Eagle
decided to fly
down

so lonely was he
for family
when he landed
upon the ground
that he touched
each red skin
he could find
then chanted alone
his final good-byes
while grieving
one ultimate time
for the unending sin
of deadly mankind

and then he was done

but when
he jumped up to fly
back to his home
in the pearly blue sky
he saw that red color run
away from its skins
and speedily come
persistently following him

so he furrowed his feathery brow
and thought what to do, and how

he decided to open a door

down deep in his soul
after screaming
one ear-splitting call
he invited that red color in

he knew in this way
he could honor forever
all
of his family dead
his sorely missed kin

that's why today
the famous Oval Office
of these United States
holds our president's seal
where Eagle stands wed
to the stars of our states

on his proud chest are placed
stripes of pure white

but between them evenly spaced
with the same number and size
fly the proud and the wide

native stripes

of indelible
red

Lothverdriel

was the magical wood
who first held them
breathing their swirling
filaments of starseed
into their first knowledge
of solid matter

'twas a forest of tightly knit
leafy canopies where sunlight
struck night shadows into daylight
releasing sweet perfumes
that rose in heated waves of blue
from off the burning noon
then fell onto never forgotten graves
in shimmering benediction to eternal life
from the smallest sentient plants
to the tallest virgin trees

the same hallowed wood
where oak and hazel
cedar and rowan
and fir and pine
all together breathed

from its many grassy clearings
twining mosses wriggled free
their tendrils giggling across
warm summer meadows
tickling the sensitive underneaths
of wildflower petals

it was the dancing emerald wood
when they had first arrived
who sealed their shining verdigris
with soft cool forest darkness
so their magic wouldn't have to dim

and it was the same wood
in long so long ago lost history
who first allowed them in

she held them then
like she holds them now
does primordial Lothverdriel
in her never ending summer spell
hidden in her crystalline
fog of bog and dell

for they were not
like you and I in there
they ate neither meat nor fruit of tree
but took their living wine from forest air
so pregnant and alive
with pranic Divine Light fare

these be
the Shining Ones
from whom we all
since have come
cycling down time's
long winding way

the Shining Ones
who still thrive there
smiling deeply into wise
and dancing Joy inside
each One of us today

Munira Judith Avinger

Author Munira Judith Avinger was born in the US and moved to the Eastern Townships of Quebec in 1992. Munira has had four books published by Borealis Press—*The Empty Bowl/Le Bol Vide*, in December 1999; *Lifting The Veil/Soulever Le Voile*, in October 2001; *Julia*, in December 2003; and *Hidden/Caché*, in November 2005.

Munira has made an in-depth study of several of the spiritual traditions of the world, including Yoga and Sufism. She has applied that study to her work as a leader of the Dances of Universal Peace. Shortly after moving to the Eastern Townships, she built a little cabin in the forest where she spends her time writing, meditating and playing music. Most of her poems have been written in this cabin.

The Night Garden

In the hush of the night garden,
I look deep into the well of tears.
I find reflected the crescent moon
and the smoldering gaze
of the red-eyed planet.

The field beyond the garden
is dark and still.
I hear crickets and the surprise
of a deer who has discovered
my presence.

I stand on a rock and survey the night.
Like Adam, I speak the names of things.
  Dark field
  Singing crickets
  Startled deer
  Red planet
  Shining moon
I pause and my words fall
into the darkness.

There are not tears enough
for the world in all its broken beauty.

I sit on the rock and close my eyes.
The moonlight shines in my mind
and I return sorrowing to You,
giver and taker of all there is.

This is Your night,
one dark blossom from the garden of nights.
I cannot ask for more.

Previously published in Hidden/Caché, *Borealis Press, Ottawa, 2005*

Quan Yin

She Who Hears
the Cries of the World

In the time of unspeakable grief,
   she waits.

Not knowing villain or victim,
   she watches.

Her arms open wide,
   invisible
   except for the light,
   which does shine through
      the dark cloud,
      the dark dream,
      the dark night,
   she listens.

Previously published in Hidden/Caché, *Borealis Press, Ottawa, 2005*

Hidden

This is sacred space,
clear pond, mirror of water,
windswept light and shadow.

Flies circle.
Frog sits in glistening curves
of greenness,
in sweet Buddha frogness,
so still beneath the Bodhi tree
of tall grass and summer seeds.

He waits for his Beloved,
who will soon come dancing,
singing on the wind,
on shimmering wing,
who will fall in gladness
to his call of longing.

This is sacred space,
opened out, swept clean –
Light, lighter than air.

Veiled by tall grass
and pond shadow,
the hidden one waits in silence.

Previously published in Hidden/Caché, *Borealis Press, Ottawa, 2005*

myamberdog

With over a 30-year history of spiritual seeking and meditation, myamberdog (Gary Hunter) was still lost on his pathless path until poetry found him at the turn of 2000, the creative urge awakening like an unpredicted emotional storm. A few years ago he gathered some of that energy and created a little book: *Pretending to be Two, Longing to be One.* And now is delighted to be contributing to this Anthology and the mission of its profits—to help educate underpriviledged children of India. He lives in the desert sands of Palm Springs with his beloved mangos, his partner Joe and two little four-legged love balls called Amber and Gracie. Gary believes poetry offers a gifted glimpse of the deeper side of absolutely everything, and carries profound gratitude for this particular group of poets/friends—a wise and caring bunch that have cultured his art and his heart. He very much supports the "endangered" creature called poetry and its mystical power to create wonder, inspire and soothe.

e-mail: myamberdog@gmail.com

fast music, slow dance

A direct look at God
might burn up your being

so we look at an infant
and melt in
increments,

at our lover and
dodge the
unquenchable coals

or at a moonrise
and reflect on
the reflection
of a raging
bonfire

sound
asleep...

She Trips over Everything He Knows

I juggle books
to keep my brain in shape

My heart is not so coordinated

In the first few steps
she trips
over
everything
he knows...

The Seeding

Outside the eternal garden,
happiness has a bloom time
I lose track of in the seeding

The blanched petal blanket
soon fades, tears apart and
falling, covers the grains
of its likeness

By then I am reeling and hide
in small locked closets
and never follow the rain into the
earth's belly or detect
any germinating young pricking,
kicking the dark patient mother...

How much of life labors
unseen in muddy dungeons like this,
our eyes accustomed
to only what glistens...?

To us,
joy is born suddenly
blind and blinding

My gaze, as always, the
excited sunlight that picks
up the ecstatic arrival
with two hands

as my hope presses the bottle
to the bent-mouthed stem
and says more to eternity
than any pleading with time,

drink... please drink... drink

Here Appeared

Here appeared
but it was Now that
touted:

"I won't ask where you've been
if you don't say 'how time flies!'

Can we just hold each other
and with our soft eyes
together, melt the
face we are
looking
through"

Stealing Myths

Where is it that time goes
and all things written
on water?

It is because my wings have stopped growing
that the sky steals my myths
without breaking a sweat

and i
for hours and hours
could observe (and do)

the conduct of butterflies
pursuing the habits of bees

but entirely nobly
and much much
more
gracefully...

The Wine of Why

Complain as they might,
crows don't sue,
daffodils decline beauty contests
and oceans will not discriminate,
kicking out whales to welcome elephants

Haven't we
been blessed with a sacred job:
harvesting togetherness,
sowing seed into a new wind?

With all this free fuel for laughter,
why duel with sharp blades
or introduce those vicious pets
we raise inside?

Remember our shining selves
lunching on mountains,

our smiles tying opinions to posts

our wonderful love pouring drinks on the house?

Your mugs, cups, glasses, please...
everyone please saddle up to the punch bowl.

this party begins with a dunking
and a toast

into the bubbling divine well
into the wine of why we are here...

Narinder Bhandari

Narinder Bhandari, 76, a retired Army Officer, lives in Chandigarh, India, with wife Ravi, son Karan and family.

The greatest 'happening' in his lifetime, says he, was the Death of Time for one single Moment in 1982; gift of his Guru, God and Meditation. Past and Future ceased to exist. Life became a spontaneous living in the Light of awareness of the present Moment.

Of that experience, narinder expresses in the following words.
"The Death of Time is the Death of the Mind.
The ensuing Silence is TOTAL.
That Silence, sudden-like, becomes a sound... a Sound
            that is itself Light... or is it the other way around...
The darkness of Mind, in throes of death, gives Birth to a
            Light so dazzling that the eyes close in ecstasy...
            and in the ears rings the Music of the following
            words...
'Anand bhaya meri Mayee, Satguru mein Paya'
('Bliss, O my Beloved mother,
The Satguru has removed the veil') between HIM and Me,
To reveal Himself to me!
Ah, BLISS, truly
Has become My Being
Narinder, now, is the Satguru's disciple!

Ah, how the Music resonates...!"

Poetry begins to arise in the Consciousness in 1998.

Words that have been heard thousands of times before are now words NO MORE. The Words are the Light. The Words are the Sound. In the poem "Seeing Is Seeing No More", Narinder tries to express the inexpressible...

Seeing Is Seeing No More

In the Timeless Zone, where Sound and Light are One
Hearing is hearing no more
Nor Seeing seeing anymore
Hearing now is the Seeing
Seeing itself is the Hearing

The Soundless Sound makes itself heard
And the Inner Ear perceives in it the Light divine
Singing songs of Love

Love
Unknowable, unknown and choiceless
Blossoming as Compassion in wondrous action
Where
Opposites are opposites no more
Right and Wrong are no more the joy of intellect!
In the embrace of Love
They choose to die forever
And all is Silent.

AUM!

AUM

One-ness, where nought was but itself
Did in its desire for expression
Manifest itself as the soundless sound
The sound of AUM

AUM, the seven notes singing in silence

AUM, the beauteous beholding of the inner eye
AUM, the honeyed delight of the Virgin tongue
AUM, the soft caress of the eternal Being
And the first fragrance of Non-being.

AUM, the One true expression of the Eternal Reality
That leads the Second back
To the Nothingness
Which is
Everything-ness.
ONE-NESS!

He Calls

Beloved,
Come into my Embrace,
Softly, silently, lovingly,
Naked, totally naked,
And feel the Joy of my
Nothingness enveloping you.

Beloved,
Sigh to me in silence,
In silence, whisper of love,
In silence, let your hands caress,
And revelling in the deep Silence that I am
Become One with me.

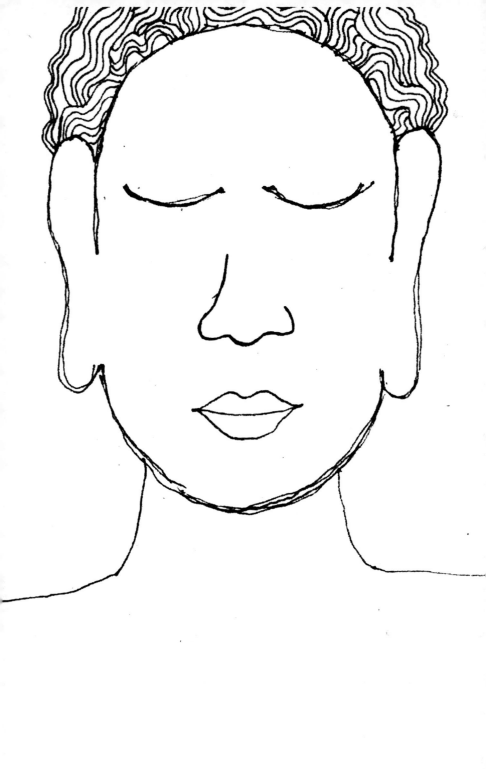

To My Friends in the Chaikhana

Dear friends,

Your words are not really words
For they arise from the Silence that Is
That just Is
Not .... the word 'Silence' .... but that which Is, just Is.
The words,
They do arise from
Your Feelings and your Thinking
Bathed in the Silence of your Being.
Burdenless.

And so, eternally, the words have been spoken
By the Knowers of The Truth
By the Buddhas
Spoken in Love
For the Seeking Heart
Groping for the Light of Love
Unborn and Unchanging.

Such is the Power of their Love
That their Words So True
Awaken the Dreamer and the Asleep
And ...
The Awake too ... They awaken!
Into expressing in words
The Song of Silence!
The Dance of Love!

Your words, my friends,

Are more Feeling than Thoughts
They lead old nari into Bliss of Being
To Bliss of Silence ... Non-Being!

Thank you, dear friends,
Your words are not really words!

narinder in Love

Priya Shah

Priya Shah lives in India.
She is an Interior & Graphic Designer by qualification and Proprietor at WEBE Enterprise - an initiative towards making 'well-being' a day-to-day concern.

www.webeorganic.in
e-mail: priyashah012@gmail.com

Confession

I am getting choked
under the burden of my dreams.
I would consider a revision
for a moment's ease.

I have no guts
to let them go
and so I stand by them,
because I think they are mine.

Like a Dog Wagging its Tail

listen
to your heart
that beats without halt
so that you may breathe
touch, love

pause, a while
and take a look...
it is eager for your glance
and is waiting,
like a dog wagging its tail.

Rock

dear rock
I am shocked to see you so dead.
let's talk.
my grandmother says that the rocks have an ability to hear...
can you hear me? dear rock?
I have a confession to make...
'I hate you'
with your rockyness
your extreme sharpness
your insensitiveness...
you are pre-occupied with your ego
all the time
and you have no time to respond back!
why were you born at all
when you had to live like dead!
emotionless...

love comes to caress you
with a perfumed zephyr;
either you are dumb
or you just don't care...

love comes to lick you
in form of raindrops;
but you dry off in a moment;
each time you refrain.

love comes to see you
in form of sun rays;
and tries hard to penetrate

but never does a flower grow.

years go by
and you are still there
unchanged
unaware
missing, the goal of living
missing, enjoying...
I pity you...

dear rock,
I have one more confession to make,
you are the best listener,
I have ever met...

As children do

we all sleep
as children do...
as we wake up
we always want to sleep a little more...
then we clean our bodies
and wear masks
of adulthood.
we become professionals,
critiques and accountants...
competitors,
winners and losers...
we discuss politics, poverty
and floods
we discuss poetry, children
and gadgets
we waste a lot of food...
we dance on a romantic tune...

later in the night
in a cozy bed
we prefer to be uncivilized,
unsophisticated and barbaric

we say a little prayer
but remain confused
and go back to sleep
as children do.

silent lotus

silent lotus is a spiritual advisor. His poetry has been published in Europe, England, America, Canada and Australia. Having resided for a significant portion of his life in the Caribbean and The Netherlands, he has retained his affiliation with the unique community of Roosevelt, NJ where he was raised. For a number of years he facilitated poetry circles at the Institute For The Study & Practice Of Nonviolence in Providence, RI. He lives with the artist Nermin Kura.

www.silentlotus.net

A Way Above

He
Spoke
Of her comfort zone
In symbolic
Haiku

She
Snapped
Her fingers
And the silence was
Pure

Apricots And A Ney

Like
Linen napkins
Stained with confessions
The snow clouds kissed the back side of the mountains
While wind currents and silver foxes howled through the night
And when again dawn dined by the riverbanks
The hinges of the swinging doors
Had been tightened

Survival

She
Survived
Like gold leaf
In an unexpected dance
Of gentle
Breeze

Her
Moment
Was

Those moments

When she gave silence
The chance to
Speak

The Oracle

She
Took my life
To her level of innocence
In the way of rain clouds
That have nothing
Left to
Say

i
fed
her
silence
with a palette knife
and let the hues
have their
way

Unhinged

The
Night
Moved on
Like a rain rolling off
Oilskin

An
Unborn
Laughter
Waited on the
Wings

There
Was purpose
In the lack of deception
And a sense of being
Without urgency to
Win

No
Need
To capture
A hint of tomorrow
Or to hold history
Hostage

It
Was
A silence
That spoke with
An indigenous vernacular
That owned no concept of
Sin

Waiting On Wagers

The
Whisper sensed
More than sensibilities
And
the village recorder
Noted seedlings
needed more than
Borrowed
Time
Foam
On the walls
Of her almost finished coffee
Resembled long ago surfaces of
Eclipsed
Moon
The
Way
Was charitable
As friends were laid to
Rest
An authentic wind and persistent
Light

smileysabu

smileysabu is a retired accountant living in the Pacific Northwest, and has been writing poetry since the sixth grade.

Today

In the morning
when I rise
before I wipe the slumber
from my eyes

It is your tender face
and the gentle warmth
of your hand that I seek

I imagined that I saw
your love rise
embracing me

Your green flecked eyes
reflecting joy back at me
the sun rose sending
brilliant light into
expectant pools

Robins and blue jays
sang the music of the spheres
and together entwined
arms, thighs
yours, mine
we two climb

Your ivory
my ebony
then we kiss
such sweet bliss

It's here we lay
for the rest of the day
eating ambrosia
and drinking wine
until we are sated
and fall asleep
to dream
of another heaven

Crystal

into our lives they come
working on each of us
trying to teach us how to become
one in consciousness
showing us who we truly are
Love and Light eternally
sometimes pathways are difficult
we fall through the heavy density of this reality
with blinders on

we regress
trees are burned and Gaia bleeds red
crystals sing as they sadly record
the records of our atrocities
in their souls they know
our hearts are beginning to awaken and see
what marvelous creators of Light we can be
so we pick up the gauntlet
to share and care
for this precious Divine spark
the crystal now grows
its luminescence increases
the world shines in the connectedness

Promise

Beloved of mine

I will be your eyes
If the light in yours begins to fade
I will be your hands
to carry what you can't
I will be your legs
and walk the long road
I will be your arms
and hold you while you sleep
you have always been my heart
and I shall love you

Steve Toth

Born in northern Minnesota. My family was snowed in after I got home from the hospital. Grew up in Eastern Iowa. Went to poetry school at the University of Iowa. Fell in love & married Sheila. With some friends started the Actualist school of poetry. Lived in Los Angeles for 27 years. Now living in northern California where the Pacific Ocean, coastal mountains & redwood forests come together.

Nothing I've Said

Some cultures have words
    that with rare exceptions
    are too holy to be uttered aloud
but I was raised in a culture
    where the only words
    you aren't supposed to say
are dirty words spoken by potty mouths
    Of course there are other words
    that mean the same things
but it is the dirty words that count
    I like it when available words take me
    places I've never been before

There are plenty of restless energies
    floating around crying for tongues
    Would-be words that try to trick you
into calling them some kind of name
    by getting personal
    "First you make up your mind"
They say with an exaggerated wink
    "like a crook makes up an alibi
    then you say one thing but do another
& after that you play favorites
    Nothing you've said has yet
    to improve upon silence"

You don't know the half of it
    I'm much worse than you think
    Sometimes language is a bell & my
mind is the clapper of its own undoing

Only the fully rung fully realize
Now before I slip on my slippers
I tap them upside down so any words
    that have crawled in will fall out
    There ought to be something
you can't forget that keeps you
    noticing how things change
    when you pay attention to them

Self-Pity

If walking around
    the house at night
you should happen
    to kick a piece
of maya hard enough
    your toenail will
    turn purple & fall off

There is no situation
    so bad that a little
self indulgent belief
    that your life is
harder & sadder
    than everybody else's
    can't make it worse

Trouble with Immunity

On the bus the subject
  of conversation turns to tales
of poison oak outbreaks
  The driver says
he found out early in life
  that poison oak has
  no effect on him

But it did cause him
  a lot of trouble once anyway
To impress a young woman
  he ate a few leaves
one thing led to another
  & she stayed the night as a lover
  but lost her temper in the morning

Her body had erupted in rashes
  She certainly didn't feel like
touching him or his sweat anymore
  So beware speculation of cause & effect
He ate the poison oak
  She made no contact
  but she woke up with the sores

Backyard Composition

Weeds bad apples
    vegetables that bolted
    peas that died happy
tall grass the mower never reaches
    flowers we deadheaded
    excess penstemon & fuchsia growth
with bumblebees still
    entering the red blossoms
    as I carry them & their nectar away

All this & more goes
    into the compost heap
    until it's almost as tall as I am
but what comes out is the same
    dirt just a little darker
    but with the same red tinge
as the dirt in the rest of the yard
    We put this new dirt
    into the gardens when we plant

There are places where before
    only weeds would grow
    & a few where even
burr clover wouldn't grow
    Now the soil grows all over
    but it gets tired
I wonder if the stuff
    our souls are made out of
    is anything like this new dirt

I know I didn't come here
    for the things we can never have
    enough of because we might
just need more in the future
    or to smell the fear in everyone's sweat
    I came here for the love
If the smoke is rising to the heavens
    & the ashes are falling to the earth
    then the fire must be you my love

Stree

I am grandfather to a beautiful 4-year-old girl, father to a grown son and daughter, husband to my wife of 30 years. I am a woodworker, I make and mend things. I have no qualifications educational, vocational or otherwise.

e-mail: christopher.keir@gmail.com

The sweetpeas today

Someone asked me, "What is joy?"

I answered,

The sweetpeas today, had the ruby velvet of a great Aunt's
    best dress,
The blue of the Norfolk sky at dawn, the sweet pink of my
    Granddaughter's cheek,
the deep cream of a young Buck's fur-covered horn,
I gazed at these with a clear sky behind,
I was lost in the wonder and the world was left ...
This is Joy, being part of the day.
This is Joy,
Being part of the Way.

If an Angel did play

You shimmered, I remember, silent in the sunlight and
        spoke to me as quietly and quite invisibly
as dawns whispers in the breeze,
sang to me through songbirds, painted pictures with the
        clouds and trees
Silent unknown You, yet always known, Who were You?
That opened me, blessed me, found me, came beside and
        made me know life
in blinding light of unfolding wonders set me free.

Did you come to see, that I could see?
to be sure I was sent my Soul...
and sent on my way?
Was it then? when I was nought but a twelvemonthling
That I was set by You, to become to Be?

Teala

I began writing sacred poetry during a difficult energetic awakening in January 2010, when I was encouraged to join the Chaikhana poetry forums by my Kundalini healer. I had long practiced in the spiritual lineages of Advaita Vedanta and more recently Tibetan Bon Dzogchen, including travelling to India four times. However Kundalini awakenings can far outstrip even the best efforts to practice, leaving one self to reckon with the soul, God, formlessly. Here poetry is both an outpouring of the mysterious language of the soul, and a path of healing. Here I have found activation of spiritual potentials, a meeting myself in the mirror of others, through the sharing of sacred poetry. You can read more poetry and articles about Kundalini healing at www.thestreamoflife.net

Vibhuti

When I met God
I threw open the doors
I did not know everywhere
He entered
Would be consumed
By fire
Especially my mind

Confused by the smoke
I wandered looking
For him that lit the blaze
Longing for that speech
That can only take place
Between the flame
And its torch

Forced to accept loss
I gave up what burned
And fell free
Life moved in slow motion
I held fast to him in nothingness
The gift of immolation so clear
But then, God raised the walls from ash
And resurrected my mind

It walks like a ghost unseen
Through hallways at work and home
I "know" these thoughts are empty
I, you and these things just do not exist
They are made only of presence

Yet God demands I speak to him
Of tomorrows and yesterdays
He hands me back an ego
And somethingness
Though I long for nothingness
And the awareness it brings

Oh I pray on bended knees
Lord, you have marked me
With the most sacred ash
Three lines across my forehead
Must I accept this damn confusion?
This ego, time and space
For this mind and the whole world
To burn completely into
Vibhuti

I am the damp, I am the wood
I am the fire, the burning, the smoke
Because you put me to the torch
I am that vibhuti

As Illusions Go

My body flows
Through me
Like this poetry
Winds through my mind

Presence holds me
All of the time

As illusions go
A dialogue with you
Is still a favorite
Of mine

Exactly What I Need to See

I feel the waves of this war
Roar
Within me
I wake up and look into the mirror
What I see
Must be me
The bondage, the coward, the tyrant
The leaders of the charge, the valiant
What I see outside of me
Is my own eternity
Spun through the looking glass
Of my heart
I pick Divinity up and put her down
Like a rag doll
Have I shaken her enough?
What doesn't seem awake
Is exactly what I need to see
To wake up

Custody Agreement

The words detail
A document
Insidious swords or
Esteemed messengers
Of cooperation
Depending on the hearts
Of those who will
Bring them home
To their children

For me
To reach
And find
Agreement
On Custody
Is a gift
Only the heavens
Can bear

I cry
For each simple step
Some now feel
So mountainous
Given where I was
I know only an angel of Love
Helped me scale these heights
To see my son's father
Through an open heart
So he now can step forward
Where before, in pain

I measured lack
And only held him back

But heaven's true gifts
Require all you have
Like a magnetic field
You walk through
Recalibrating your
Every direction
Accepting karmic winds
Of others' into your soul
Once more
For you all to do more
Than just survive

And
There are those
That have called this agreement
Bullshit
Nearly rending my opened heart in two
Again
Oh, and do I rise up
To release
This insidious poison
They offer my soul
Why here in this culture
Is division worshipped
Even if it is literally killing you?

Wildfire

Precious Gem

a precious stone
wet...

blue green...

a single planet spins its stories
arcing through
this
trackless
space
wherein
all worlds
are born...

and die...

circling
round some molten core...

that scale
time's
ancient order
in their cycles...

numberless orbs
ejecting
shattered splinters
of dioptric light
that shear
the dark

and radiate the eons...

until at last...
within obsidian night
they coalesce
to form
a canopy
of jewels...

faint
shimmering
points
hidden from each downcast eye
until...

by grace...

a man lifts heavenward
his gaze
to see
in stricken
awe
such beauty
measured out beyond the compass
of
his
mind

...

yet
all these wonders
that pass before
the sight
of man
and are but a
burst of brilliance
refracted
from
a facet
of this...

most precious gem...

suspended
in the
void...

of
consciousness...

this single eye
that headless sees
all life
as the image of
omniscience...

whose ear
alone
resounds

to the chorus
of each creature's cry...

and the music of
the
dance...

inhaling
scent of sacrifice...

of those who suffer...

savouring
too...

their
joy

glowing
with heat of passion...

enfolded
in the
womb
of
Love's
Beloved...

Love

One Love

without turning...

I face these... the cardinal points of My being...

north and south
east and west

above and below...

without moving...

I traverse this Heartland
of desire...

flesh of My flesh
blood of My blood...

sacrificed upon these fires:

age and disease...

accident
and murder...

the smoke of their pyred corpses
mingling
with
the perfume
of My Being...

leaving not a trace...

how few I know
who die... before they die...
who know Me...

as

I am...

and fewer still...

who
before they die

are joined

as Lover and Beloved...

in

this

One

Love

Love's Embrace

vision shining...

Seeing her reflected
against the dark cold void...

enshrouded by grey mist
of Vulcan's fumes
hot lava of her blood...
pouring forth
to fertilise the seed of life...

ahh... Beloved

algae breathing the first breath
upon an ancient shore

bringing into being
life in abundance...

dolphins playing flying
from water into air
a leap of joy...

bear and wolf
and fallow deer...

prowling...

startled...

death at her throat

and in her final sacrifice
bare thigh and breast
exposed...

tasting her milk...

sweet fruits and savoury meat...

heady wine
of Love's embrace...

Love

Adieu

The senses are My palette
painting images
of
life

upon this
clear
still
void...

each brush stroke
paints the world

and in an instant

wipes the canvass
clean...

leaving
not a trace
of paint
upon
this
faceless face...

of

Love

Empowering Literacy
Our Path of Charitable Giving

All proceeds from the sale of this book of poetry will be donated to the Ninash Foundation, a 501 © (3) charity that promotes literacy among female and minority children of India. Since 1996, Ninash, with the assistance of SUNY Oneonta students and others from the USA, has built six Indo-International schools, which are providing education to more than 1200 underprivileged children of India. These schools have been making a genuine economic and cultural impact on the three villages in which they are located. As hubs of educational and social change, Ninash-funded schools stand out as a model for the rest of rural India. This exciting progress in rural Indian education has been made possible by generous donations from all over the world. To continue providing neglected Indian children with access to education and a future, the Ninash Foundation needs to raise $60,000 annually to cover our school salaries and other expenses. Consequently, Ninash continues to make an appeal each year to generous individuals and organizations to join the team and become partners in promoting literacy among the underprivileged. Their gift to rural Indian education is like "the giving tree," which will keep giving for generations to come. Donations can be sent to the Ninash Foundation, 17 Center Street, Oneonta, New York, 13820, USA, and through PayPal at www.ninash.org. Many thanks to all the contributors to this poetry anthology for generously donating the proceeds from the sale of this book to the Ninash Foundation.

Dr. Ashok Kumar Malhotra, founder and president, and
Linda Marie Drake, treasurer, of the Ninash Foundation

CPSIA information can be obtained at www.ICGtesting.com
Printed in the USA
LVOW07s1036191115

463088LV00005B/18/P